# Our Waiting Is God's Working

### By Missy Grant

*"Attempt something so impossible that unless God is in it, it's doomed to failure."*
*~John Haggai*

**Our Waiting is God's Working**
by Missy Grant

ISBN 9781092374897

© Missy Grant 2019

Published in the United States

All rights reserved. No portion of this book may be reproduced, stored in a retrieval system, or transmitted in any form or by any means – electronic, mechanical, photocopy, recording, scanning, or other – without prior written permission of the publisher. Self Published with KDP.Amazon.com. Email questions to missygrant49@gmail.com.

Picture on front cover website is pokrie@icloud.com

# Table of Contents

Table of Contents ............................................................................. 3
Acknowledgements ......................................................................... 5
What Others are Saying .................................................................. 7
Introduction ..................................................................................... 9
## YOU ........................................................................................... 10
### SPIRITUAL ............................................................................... 11
So Much More .............................................................................. 11
Wonderfully Messy ....................................................................... 13
Be Like A Child ............................................................................ 15
What is Your Golden Statue? ....................................................... 17
What To Remember When Waiting And Wounded ..................... 19
Laboring In Prayer ........................................................................ 21
All She Can Do Is Laugh .............................................................. 22
### MENTAL .................................................................................. 24
A Change, A Tweak, Or An Overhaul .......................................... 24
Small But Mighty .......................................................................... 26
Bury Fear With Faith .................................................................... 28
Adoption Is Absolutely A Battleground ....................................... 30
Ready, Set, False Start .................................................................. 32
Well Of Water ............................................................................... 34
### EMOTIONAL ........................................................................... 36
Better Now Than Later ................................................................. 36
Clear As Mud ................................................................................ 38
Forward Focused ........................................................................... 40
Heard By God ............................................................................... 41
### PHYSICAL ............................................................................... 42
Physical Health Is Your Catalyst .................................................. 42
Permissible Is Not Always Beneficial .......................................... 44
Turn North ..................................................................................... 46
Sustain It! ...................................................................................... 48
Sometimes You Just Have To Flee! .............................................. 50
Everybody's Got One! ................................................................... 52
## MARRIAGE ............................................................................... 54
The Litmus Test ............................................................................ 55
Small Fractures Lead To Big Cracks ............................................ 57
"Fix Or "Fit" .................................................................................. 59
A Devoted "I Will Go" Love ........................................................ 61

Really What It's All About..................................................................63
## YOUR ADOPTED CHILD..................................................65
Huge Mosaic Of Redemption ............................................................66
A Unique Path....................................................................................68
Why The Anger?................................................................................70
Tiny Seeds..........................................................................................72
## YOUR CURRENT FAMILY..............................................76
High Investment Now=High Return Later .........................................77
Pride Can Be Subtle ...........................................................................79
Did She Really Say That?!.................................................................81
Always Upside Down ........................................................................83
Freed For A Purpose ..........................................................................84
## OTHER PEOPLE................................................................86
Cul-De-Sac Christianity.....................................................................87
Who Are You Listening To?..............................................................89
Triumphal Parade...............................................................................91
A Fragrant Life ..................................................................................93
In Closing...........................................................................................95
A Note From The Author...................................................................96
Sources and Quotes............................................................................97

# *Acknowledgements*

Thank you to the incredible staff of Lifeline Children Services that encouraged me to write and prompted this devotional book . We began this together in 2014 and you have persevered with me through many stops and starts! Levacy, Beth, and many others…you know who you are. I am humbled and grateful to be aligned with a ministry that seeks Christ first. I have witnessed this as an adoptive parent of two, and also as a laborer and advocate for vulnerable children and families all over the world"

Thank you Jenny and Jefferson, my reasons behind my passion for writing TRAILS FOR TICOS… and now for OUR WAITING IS GOD'S WORKING. You encouraged me to write, even if that meant our outdoor time together was cut short. May you always whole-heartedly Pursue with reckless abandon the One-Who calls us by name and adopted us and into His forever family. I love you like the moon and the stars.

Thank you Patrick, my husband of twenty, for encouraging me to press on when I was tempted to let the words only stay in my head with this whole book idea! You didn't let me get bogged down in the details, but saw the bigger picture. Thank you, I love you to the ends.

Thank you mom, the true wind beneath my wings and my best friend. If I had an agent, you would be the first and last! You bought more Trails for Ticos books than I did-and I'm confident you gave them all away! I love you and dad (who is dancing with Jesus) more than words. And Carol, my mom's identical twin and my mom #2, you have encouraged every writing piece I have done! -thank you. You too, are such an inspiration, and I love you.

Thank you to all who followed my blog and first book TRAILS FOR TICOS and who encouraged me to continue writing. Your enthusiasm and encouragement was contagious! You truly encouraged this athlete and exercise physiology major, whose writing experience consisted of a simple love for journaling, to write and keep writing, for a bigger purpose.

Thank you Jeanne Saul, my saving grace, my gift from the Lord publisher and editor, who I'm not totally convinced is a human and not an angel since we have never actually met in person! You have been my queen navigator through BOTH books. You are such a gift!

Thank you Katie Bonner, my volunteer editor and far away life-long friend…you helped tweak my words when they needed tweaking! I'm so grateful and I hope to be able to return the favor for your book one day!

# *What Others are Saying*

## About "Our Waiting is God's Working"

Missy Grant is as real as real can be. I had the privilege of sharing life with Patrick and Missy before, during, and after the adoption of their two children, and was always inspired by Missy's simple and persistent faith. In writing these devotions, Missy is opening her heart and sharing the gold she's found through firsthand experience as an adoptive parent. What a gift!
*Christa Wells-singer, song writer and winner of 2006 Dove award songwriter of the year.*

This devotional will be such a gift for families in the waiting stage of adoption. Missy does a beautiful job pursuing the heart of the reader while pointing them to the heart of God.
*Jennifer Phillips-adoptive parent and author of "BRINGING LUCY HOME" and "30 Days of Hope for Adoptive Parents" books*

Missy Grant has walked through this firsthand and can testify all the Lord can do in the life of an adoptive parent, a child, and a family as a whole. It has been a true joy and honor to witness this personally in the life of the Grant family as their adoption social worker and now friend. The Lord's love is truly evident in the Grant family, and we rejoice with them in the ways the Lord uses them daily to impact their community around them. Wherever you are in the adoption journey, remember that adoption is a marathon and not a sprint. The Lord is faithful and will give you all the grace needed to walk through each step of the journey.
*Beth Perez-Lifeline Children Services Latin America Program Director*

Missy Grants devotional, *Our Waiting is God's Working* is a great encouragement of God's love and pursuit of us even as we wait. Using her own experience of adoption and life experiences, she

challenges and reminds us, through scripture that God is at work continuously in our lives preparing us for the journey ahead.
*Karen Bowen-a wonderful and wise friend*

Adoption is not easy, but God doesn't always call us to easy. Adoption is a glorious picture of the Gospel; and because of that, Satan goes to war against it. In *Our Waiting is God's Working*, Missy Grant fortifies our faith by leading us to the truth and promises of God's Word. All who are seeking to care for orphaned or vulnerable children will find help and hope in these pages.
*David Wooten-Lifeline Children Services Florida Director*

Throughout the pages of this devotional, Missy beautifully explores the depth of struggles in light of the cross. She is honest and vulnerable as she shares the hope and peace she has found in Jesus Christ. I highly recommend this book to not only adoptive families, but to everyone seeking a lifeline in the midst of challenges. You will find that each scripture-filled page is like a breath of fresh air which will leave you rejuvenated and ready to face another day.
*Twila Miles, friend, adoptive mother, artist, and author of "Whispers of Hope: Finding Perspective Post Adoption"*

# *Introduction*

Waiting... Delayed gratification... These "activities" are probably not on most people's bucket list. Before we discount them altogether, maybe we just need to reframe them. With our eyes wide open, we are likely to find many hidden treasures along the way. In Christ, we have already been lavished with the costliest and most precious gift of all! Once orphans, (yes, we were ALL orphans until Christ rescued us!) we are now royal sons and daughters of the Almighty because Christ allows us to exchange our dirty rags for His royal robes. Truly, is there anything better than going from "orphan" status to "child of the King" status?!

If you are reading this book, you are probably in some stage of waiting in your adoption journey, or in your life. My hope and prayer in writing this book is multifaceted. May this time be so much more than words on a page.

I pray that this devotional book will illuminate the height and the depth of our Savior's love for you like only His Spirit can do. It is written in ordered sections, but you will want to approach each section with your Bible and notebook and possibly your colored pencils in hand, giving yourself the freedom of time (more or less) as you feel is needed. Starting by reading the Scriptures. Some sections might encourage your soul, while others might lead to soul-searching challenge and conviction. Humbly approach each day in bold expectancy of His Spirit to work! Wait confidently and intently on Him, as you are waiting for your precious child (or whatever you are waiting for). Everybody's footprint and parenting journey is uniquely different, but each one shares challenges and victories. Find your solid footing as you look to Jesus, the One in whom we live, move, and have our being (Acts 17:28).

# YOU

# SPIRITUAL

*Let this section be your springboard for all other sections.*

## So Much More

**Scripture:** Philippians 1:6, Proverbs 3:5-6, Isaiah 55:9

**Key Idea**: As you embark on this waiting journey, be confident that this waiting process can be so much more than simply waiting. Know that you are not alone. Many other faithful servants have walked a similar road in pursuit of responding to God's call. Let's immerse our thoughts and hearts together as we diligently seek the One on the throne who never sleeps or slumbers. The One who is always at work. Our God is never dormant. His presence and power are always at work, even in ways that we may never see, especially on this side of heaven. Our understanding is limited and our comprehension is faulty, but we see glimpses and pieces of Him as we seek Him and bask in His Word. As we embark on the first day of our journey together, let's frame everyday forward from this vantage point: It is God's amazing love that pursued and rescued us (past tense), pursues and rescues us (present tense), and came and comes for us (past and present tense). He is called the Father of the fatherless for a reason (Psalm 68:5) He sacrificed everything to claim us as His children. May this continued awareness pry open the eyes of our heart and remove the cobwebs of complacency. One visual that helped to rid me of complacency in our waiting process was seeking to view the wait through the gaze of a trapeze flyer. I realize this might be a stretch (literally!), but the mind is a powerful tool. Think back to your last circus attendance; remember how the trapeze artist seemingly swung back and forth forever, while preparing for the catch. Indefinitely, yet also intentionally, the swinger decides, at some pivotal point, that it's time...time to let go. Well, that's about where you are in this waiting journey right?! Trust the timing as you release and let go, and enter into this vague, unfamiliar, exciting - yet out of your control-time frame. It is not quite time for your catch, as two seemingly contradictory things are taking place: you are in motion; but, yet you are still, so that you do not accelerate the catch. You wait in absolute trust and must not flail about in anxiety… you are moving, yet somewhat still. While waiting for your catch, the air around you is filled with a lot of adoption preparation. Will you allow this precious time to be so much more than just waiting? In many ways, what you let God do in you during this wait is a vital piece of what He will do through you when your child comes home. (Jeannie I took the "home" sentence away) Remember that trust is only as strong as the object being trusted. The great CATCHER is absolutely worthy of your trust.

**Reflection:** Begin your journey with a time of prayer. *Lord God our Father, we praise You for seeking us out and adopting us as your children. We will never be able to comprehend or deserve Your unfathomable love made possible to us through our Savior Jesus Christ. Increase our longing for You as we depend on Your faithfulness. Thank you that our salvation does not depend on our faithfulness, but on You alone. Increase our faith as we seek You through every page of this book. Thank you for what you are doing, and thank You ahead of time, for what You will continue to do. Give us a patient and hopeful trust as we seek You, our great Catcher. In Your Name alone we trust and rest.*

# *Wonderfully Messy*

**Scripture:** 1 Samuel 2, Isaiah 61:3

**Key idea:** In the adoption world, and in life, we know that our time table and God's time table are often at opposite sides of the spectrum! We are a society obsessed with productivity and efficiency. Obviously, productivity is positive and beneficial in many ways, but somewhere along the way, instant gratification has become an obsession. The implication of the word 'wait' is that of a four-letter word that makes our skin crawl. Pause for a moment, if you would, and simply remind yourself that God unabashedly pursued you as His child. He knows your going out and your coming in, and He knows every detail that will come to pass in your family's adoption story. This waiting time can become a sacred journey, one that pries deeper into God's loving heart, while also into your own. As you embark on this soul-searching journey with open hands, pray for clarity and embrace perspective shifts that may arise. When we try to rush God (as if God could be rushed), we will always end up disappointed because God's plan is ultimately what we really need and desire. In our impatient moments, we want the quick fix, the immediate answer, the "efficient" way. We know of many great men and women in the Bible who can more than relate. Hannah is a great example of a woman who experienced great turmoil, yet also great reward in the Lord. God honored her commitment and used her mightily during a dark historical period. Though once heartbroken and barren, God transformed beauty from ashes when Hannah gave birth to Samuel. God used Samuel as a mighty judge and prophet, who played a pivotal role in turning the nation of Israel back to Himself.

Your adoption is so much more than bringing your child(ren) home, although that is beautiful in and of itself. Your adoption is about what He wants to do — and will do — IN and THROUGH you and everyone involved. We show God that He is the sole source of our hope as we willingly let go of our agenda. St. Augustine reminds us that God made us for Himself, and "our hearts will be restless until they find their rest in God". Hannah found rest as she poured her heart out before the Lord.

**Reflection**: How can you focus less on efficiency and more on encountering God? What can you learn from Hannah? How can you rest in God, who brings beauty and hope, and turns our messes into messages?

# *Be Like A Child*

**Scripture:** Matthew 18:1-6 and 19:14

**Key idea:** Jesus often referred to children as beautiful examples of the faith and humility necessary to become part of His kingdom. The faith of a child is full of trust and loyalty, while the humility of a child is dependent and submissive. I love that Jesus tells, even requires, adults to become like children in our posture before the Lord. Concerning matters of faith, He tells adults to become like children, instead of telling children to become like adults. As adults, we often make things more complicated than they really are. In reality, all that we are promised is right now. Maybe you need this reminder as much as I do… all God wants you to do is what is in front of you…no more, no less! God promises us grace for each moment. Just like we advise our children to trust us with childlike simplicity, God wants the same for us. We will absolutely become overwhelmed if we attempt to become a historian (past dweller), a prophet (future predictor), or an expert "contraster" (where we compare our experiences with others). We have to let go of the ways we think our life should look like at this moment, and avoid comparing the way God is working in our life with the way He is working in our friend's life.

It is only when we become like a little child, completely dependent on Him moment by moment, that we are able to fully embrace Him with an "all in" mentality. Jesus welcomes, praises, and even seeks out little children! When we seek Him 'all-in' a great loss occurs — we lose our kingdom of control and independence. But, our loss is indeed great gain, because we gain His kingdom of trust and dependence. Paul Miller refers to this as moving from being "independent players to dependent lovers."

**Reflection:** Child-like trust is such a beautiful thing! How can you become more like a child by moving from independence and trusting in self to dependence on Christ?

# *What is Your Golden Statue?*

**Scripture:** Exodus 20 and James 1:17

**Key idea:** We may not have a golden statue cascading in our living room that we pay our daily respect to, but think for a moment about the things that occupy a big chunk of your mental space. Where do you spend most of your time? Where do your thoughts roam when doing menial tasks? An idol can be a person, place, or anything that serves as a "go to" when we encounter stress. We know that we are serving an idol when we love the gifts of God more than we love the God Who gives these gifts. We can even make idols out of good things like adoption, spouses, children, or our God-given talents or strengths. Idols often originate from good "socially acceptable" things, and this can make them even more deceptive when they are good gifts from our loving Creator. But even the good gifts can detract and distract us from the One who gives us life, breath, and sustenance. If you are anything like me, you may release the people and things you love over to God's capable hands — for a short time — only to take them back quickly into your own incapable hands if/when you don't like the results. Like the Israelites, God gives us grace after grace as we continue to battle with idolatry. He is, however, a jealous God zealous for our affection. Because His love for us knows no bounds, He knows that our search for acceptance, meaning, significance, and pleasure cannot be quenched with any earthly thing or person. He wants us to enjoy His gracious gifts without elevating them to an idolatrous 'we must have.' (or idolatrous 'must haves.' - depends if you want singular or plural). The law of diminishing returns is **always** in full force in idol worship. Idolatry is a vicious cycle that always leads to more idolatry. In our reading for today, the Israelites were literally in the presence of God one minute and, in seemingly the next minute, they turned away and worshiped a statue. Before we turn up our nose and say "how in the world could they do that," let's examine our own hearts. True, we may not have a golden idol in our living room, but what or who is on our throne? Is it God on the throne?

**Reflection:** What role is the Cross of Jesus playing in your life? What is your "go to" during this waiting time? Is there anything that makes you anxious at the thought of giving it up? Take a moment in prayerful praise to the God who is the giver of every good gift, and ask Him for the eyes to see if anything needs to come down from your throne.

# *What To Remember When Waiting And Wounded*

**Scripture:** Numbers 14:11-35, 2 Corinthians 4:17-18, Hebrews 10:23

**Key idea:** Are you tired of waiting? Do you feel wounded? Be encouraged — God says that the wounded and worn out are His righteousness! I don't know about you, but I am thankful that we serve a God who is faithful. When I feel somewhat worn out with waiting, I try to remind myself not to doubt in the dark of night what I know to be true in the morning light. It is so easy to forget how faithful God is when life seems dark and God seems silent. God repeatedly tells the Israelites to "remember" His faithfulness. He is urging them to remember and to recount examples of His character as they waited. We know that the Israelites were anything but strangers to waiting. After being freed from captivity, God led the Israelites on a journey to the Promised Land. They didn't know exactly where they were going, and their circumstances were rough. Even though God told them He was taking them to an amazing place, the people grumbled and complained about conditions along the way. The ingratitude in their hearts overflowed to their mouths – and God noticed. The Israelites discovered how serious God is about complaining and grumbling.

Two to four years of adoption waiting feels like forever, but it pales in comparison to 40 years; right? When we simply praise Him for who He is and His character, we will naturally overflow into praise for what He has done, and what He will continue to do. Each recall can revive us as it leads to discovery and praise. Remembering His Hand in all of life provides the needed perspective to praise Him right where we are. We all have the tendency to be selective in our memories, and therefore it is essential that we are intentional in what we rehearse and remember.

God longs for us to trust Him completely in all of the preparation, the activity, and even in the quietness of our waiting. Hold fast and unswervingly to Him in a dependent trust, confident that God is using and redeeming every waiting moment for His glory.

**Reflect:** Where do you need to remind yourself of God's faithfulness to your striving heart? Recount and write down where God has been faithful in the past, and in your past? Take some time here, as the great "Refiner" may providentially have you wait on Him for His answer!

# *Laboring In Prayer*

**Scripture:** Luke 18:1-8, 1Thessalonians 5:18, Hebrews 7:24-26

**Key idea:** The humble posture of laboring in our prayers shows our dependence on God. When we humbly labor in our prayer life, God infuses a spirit of persistence and gratitude. When we are being stretched, our fleshly response is often to complain. But if we let the stretching lead us to labor in persistent and thankful prayer, our dependence shifts from self to God. This allows us to see how small our problems are compared to the size of our God. If we look at our Thessalonians verse for today, we are told to give thanks IN all things, and not necessarily FOR all things. We can always praise the character of God, even when we find it difficult to give thanks for a particularly difficult circumstance. When we persistently give thanks in the good, the bad, and the ugly circumstances, the scales fall from the "eyes" of our hearts.

God tells us that if we knock continually, we will receive. Our persistent knocking sets us up to receive a priceless and immeasurable gift…more of Him! Left to ourselves, we are just like the widow in Luke 11, powerless and without resources. She shows us what laboring in prayer looks like. Notice that she didn't pester Jesus, but she pressed into Jesus. This pressing filled her with power! Similarly, as we press into Jesus, He not only hears us, but He pleads alongside of us- as our High Priest. Oh, for more grace to press into our Priest and receive His power!

**Reflect:** As you spend some time in today's passages, praise Him for being on the throne, and allow yourself the gift of pressing into Him with your struggles.

# *All She Can Do Is Laugh*

**Scripture:** Genesis 18:1-15, Isaiah 43:19

**Key idea:** Todays reading takes us to the story of Sarah. The Bible tells us that she is around 100 years old, which is just more proof that God always gets the first and last word!

In our Genesis passage, we can almost hear Sarah laughing when God tells her that she will bear a child. It's probably safe to assume that her laughter was anything but giddy, but instead had a sarcastic tone to it. Can you relate to a moment of "oh my goodness Lord...now...really"?! You can almost feel Sarah's flesh crying out to God, as He appears to be showing up... late. Sarah and Abraham surely could not predict God's timing, and neither can we. God is never late, of course, but our limited and faulty viewpoint often tells us otherwise. In today's Scripture, God is reminding His people not to fear, during a time where they were scattered among the nations. He assures them of His presence as they walk through fires and floods. He even promises to gather His sons and daughters from all over the world so that He can be glorified. The Lord tells His people that He is doing something new and for them to have faith in His provision. He is more than capable of creating rivers in the desert when there is not even a drop of water in site. He did it then, and He can do it for you now. He provides for our needs in the driest and darkest places. How wonderful that He calls us to Himself and that we, like Sarah and the Israelites, get to be the recipients of His indwelling?!

This is a miracle in and of itself. You are most likely experiencing a flux of emotions in the waiting. Know that He is with you. You may be "laughing" like Sarah, wondering what God is up to; or you may be like the Israelites, caught in the spin cycle of obedience and rebellion. Wherever you are, waiting can stop us in our tracks, make us feel inadequate, and flood us with self-doubt. Trust that God is with you every step of the way. Join the ranks of Sarah, and the multitude of mighty, yet broken followers who have gone before you. God is with you through the desert, the fire, and the floods. He is also with your precious child, and all the children who are waiting for their forever home. Remember — as you are waiting, you are not the only one waiting. Countless children, including your own, are also waiting. Pray diligently for them, and for God to consume them with His presence, as He also consumes you.

**Reflect:** Can you relate to Sarah and Abraham? How is this waiting time bringing you to the end of yourself? As you are seeking Him, pray for the millions of children globally to be filled with the God of hope, and for families to rise up and answer the call to care for them.

# MENTAL

*Allow the Spiritual section you just completed to be your springboard into the following Mental, Emotional, and Physical sections. The Spiritual aspect is your big rock in the jar that needs to be in place before the smaller (but important) rocks are placed in their proper perspective.*

## *A Change, A Tweak, Or An Overhaul*

**Scripture:** Hebrews 13:8, James 1:5

**Key idea:** Allow the Spiritual section you just completed to be your springboard into the following Mental, Emotional, and Physical sections. The Spiritual aspect is your big rock in the jar that needs to be in place before the smaller (but important) rocks are placed in their proper perspective.

We know that change is one of the great constants in life. Spirit. We also know that external changes can happen quickly and are often out of our control, while internal, heart changes are usually more delicate and time consuming, happening from the overflow of our cooperation with His Thankfully, the Bible provides two great promises about change. First, our God never changes — He is the same yesterday, today, and forever. Second, our God is in the business of heart change, calling us to repentance and growth through changing our hearts. When we turn **from** our sin and **towards** our gracious Father, we start to experience victory over areas that are hindering us. Prayerfully approach this mental section as a self-detective. God may convict you of some particular sin, or He may simply be wanting you to assess your present top priorities in lieu of life changes on your horizon. It is okay to be uncomfortable! God's love is so deep for His children; He allows and wants us to be uncomfortable so that we notice and respond to others who are hurting and needy.

**Reflection:** What are your top priorities — things you are currently saying "yes" to? Sometimes we say yes to good, but less important priorities, sidetracking us from the people and things that are most important. Every choice, every "yes", always comes with a "no" to something else. Perhaps one of your yes's needs to be traded for a higher value. Remember…no wallowing in guilt …we all have unnecessary mental clutter. This is simply a perfect time to clear some of it out by changing, tweaking, or perhaps completely overhauling.

# *Small But Mighty*

**Scripture:** Judges 6:1-40, 1Samuel 17:31-51

**Key idea**: Do you ever feel like an even smaller version of David fighting big giants like Goliath? Or, maybe you feel small like Gideon, who referred to himself as the "least" in his family". In our human eyes, we often view our smallness as negative and limiting, but if we look closely, we see that our God-given limits can be the means for us to reach our full spiritual potential. Gideon might have felt small, but God referred to him as a "mighty warrior".

Our reading for today underscores the following scene: Fearing the Midianites, Gideon is afraid to winnow his wheat out in the open air, where the breeze catches the grain and separates it from the chaff. He is afraid of doing that and becoming too visible to enemy eyes. As a result, we find him crouching down, trying to thresh his wheat in the pit of a winepress. Suddenly the angel speaks to him. He probably jumped out of his skin! Referring to himself as "the least" likely meant that Gideon was economically and/or socially one of the poorest members in his tribe. Using modern terminology, we would say he was from the wrong side of the tracks. This passage paints a picture of Gideon as shy, reserved, and very unassertive. Then why did the Lord very pointedly call Gideon a "mighty warrior" (verse 12)? According to Tim Keller, God was probably prompting Gideon to get in touch with his own potential by reminding Gideon of His power in Gideon's life. In verse 14, God tells him to be strong in the confidence that God was not only with him, but was sending him. Thus, Gideon's recipe for success is the same as ours — God's indwelling and calling align with our God-given strengths to assure us of victory. Allowing our thoughts to go to extremes always takes us down a slippery path. If we forget that we are sinful, we can become overconfident and judgmental. If, on the other hand, we forget how accepted and loved we are in Christ, we will become anxious, guilt-ridden, and small. God helped Gideon in his unbelief, and He will help you.

Ralph Waldo Emerson said, "What lies behind us and what lies before us are tiny compared to what lies within us." But, if we are in Christ, we take Emerson's beliefs deeper — what lies behind us and before us are tiny because of WHO resides within us.

**Reflection:** What might God want **you** to do, while He does what **He** wants to do in you?

# *Bury Fear With Faith*

**Scripture:** Psalm 56, 2 Corinthians 5:7, Luke 18:27

**Key idea:** There is a reason "do not fear" is the most repeated phrase in Bible. True courage is not the absence of fear, but the means by which we face our fear. Our gracious Father knows that the only remedy for our fears is to turn to Him in faith. Fear is subjective, and experienced by everyone in different ways and for different reasons, but we all struggle with it to some degree. We have already addressed some fears, but other common ones are: Fear of change, fear of people, fear of the unknown, or even a fear that this whole adoption is going to crash and burn. We serve a God that knows we will have fear, and Who brings comfort in the midst of them. It is no accident that the phrase "do not fear" is in the Bible 365 times- one per day!

In his book Knowing God, JJ Packer says, "your faith will not fail while God sustains it; you are NOT strong enough to fall away because God is resolved to hold you". Nobody embodies and captures the facets of fear and faith quite like David in the Psalms. In Psalm 56 David has been captured by the Philistines and he starts to be afraid, but notice the shift when sets his sights on his Savior. In spite of his feelings, he turned his mind to praising God for being his faithful provider. David's self-talk, "WHEN I am afraid, I WILL trust in You" inspire us to live out our faith even when our emotions are in opposition. Although we may not be fleeing for our life like David was, our fears can take our minds in a thousand different directions- if we let them. Wherever we land, there is only one successful remedy. We turn and run to the One Who is well acquainted with — but not limited by — our every emotion. He graciously gives us everything we need to courageously walk by faith!

**Reflection:** Synonyms for fear include: anxiety, angst, despair, dismay, hopeless, doubt. Which of the following antonyms for fear encourage you the most: faith, assurance, calmness, contentment, trust, courage, fervent, persevering (feel free to add your own). Thank God for His empathy and His remedy in the midst of our struggles. Where do you need Him to infuse courage to you? He is working right now on behalf of your child.

# *Adoption Is Absolutely A Battleground*

**Scripture:** Joshua 1:6-9 Ephesians 6:10-11, 2 Corinthians 2:11

**Key idea:** Adoption is kingdom work, eternally impacting the kingdom for God's glory! Adoption is also a battleground and we must enter the battle prepared, because we know that good preparation is essential for any victory. Good preparation assumes that we know who/what we are fighting against, and what their goals entail. Anytime we are doing something for God's eternal glory, we can be certain that our opposition and enemy (satan) is always on a seek and destroy mission to foil our plans. It may be a gory battle, but we rejoice in knowing the end result is always in our favor, and that we are always on the winning team! Having God on the throne as the ultimate Victor allows us to trust and exhale! Yes, we exhale, but we never drop our guard! If satan is unable to completely thwart our plans, he may work overtime trying to discourage us. Take heart and remember that God is pursuing your child in the same way that He is pursuing you. God's hands are never bound by evil and nothing happens without His permission.

We see in our reading today that Moses confidently told Joshua of God's faithfulness because he had experienced it firsthand. Caleb, in turn, didn't waver, because he knew that God called them to the land, and he trusted that God would deliver on His promises. Similarly, God reminds us that there is no promised land without a wilderness, so when we are in in a wilderness, He promises to be with us. His presence gives us the strength to press on through our headwind. Press on, even if other people are doubting. Press on, even if circumstances seem daunting. Press on! As God's beloved children, we have the invaluable gift of being able to start with the end in mind! Our enemy shrinks when God's Truth is spoken and applied, making it imperative that we speak the God's truth to his lies. We also need to speak God's truth to our (more subtle) enemies of self, others, and the world. Truly, we have this ironclad cure in our battles: God won't desert us in our hour of need because we have been bought with too high a price. We may not feel completely prepared, and we may stumble, but here's the deal: NO ONE is perfectly ready or fully prepared all the time! Our Redeemer is aware of this, and He will not let us fail!

**Reflection:** How does this passage encourage you to look for Gods Hand in a world that seems to be unraveling at the seams. Where are you in the battle, and how can you start right here- in the thick of your waiting- with the end in mind?

# *Ready, Set, False Start*

**Scripture:** Romans 8:28-30, Psalm 138, Isaiah 43:1-and 55:8-9

**Key idea:** The adoption world often consists of false starts and road bumps. The process can feel like an unpredictable roller-coaster ride. You may be knee-deep in paperwork, or you may have to submit (what feels like) the same form-again and again! You may even have to back up a few steps. Rest assured, even the steps backward are forward steps in His hands, as God is weaving His redemptive story in each of you. The "almost but not yet" phase of waiting can be so challenging. In her book ONE THOUSAND GIFTS, Ann Voskamp reminds us that "when we can't see God's Hand, we can always trust His heart". When circumstances look totally different than we think they should, we remind ourselves that nothing is random with God. There are no accidents, oops, or ways to catch God off guard. The false starts and steep hikes just make for a more spectacular views from the top. Blessings are often bittersweet, and God's blessings do not exclude us from bruises, bumps, and false starts along the way. God knows we need both the bitter and the sweet, so that we trust Him alone. He seeks to turn us from a shallow trust, that only clings to victories and good things, to a deeper trust, that clings to Him even in the question marks. We can always praise Him for His character even as we struggle to praise Him in the circumstantial bumps along the way. God does not place us anywhere by accident, and He tells us to expect adversity! This waiting time is part of the process, and builds stamina for future challenges. Whether you are a new or veteran parent, changes and false starts are inevitable, each one requiring its own unique does of stamina. Why not use the waiting and false starts to pray…not only for your own and your loved one's stamina, but also for the millions of children across the globe who do not have a family to call their own. Pray for

God's relentless grace to fall on them, for their protection, and for His people to rise up and care for them.

**Reflection:** Although the "promised land" is not here yet, where can you see His faithfulness in the midst of bumps and false starts? If you are having trouble, think of that document you signed the other day, and how that is one step closer to bringing your child home. Every step counts!

# *Well Of Water*

**Scripture:** Genesis 16, Psalm 78:13-16

**Key idea:** Barren hearts (and barren wombs) are the places where God's well of water fills, sustains, fills, and even gushes. In our Genesis passage, we find Hagar at a point of complete desperation, literally about to watch her only son die for a lack of water. Shunned and completely alone, she closed her eyes and desperately cried out to the Lord. God "saw" Hagar, opened her eyes, and told her to get up because He was NOT FINISHED with her son (or her) yet! Can you imagine the sense of elation, even shock, that she felt when she opened her eyes?! Right before her eyes, in the middle of the desert, "appeared" a well of water, and the reassuring voice of God-promising strength to her son Ishmael. God was showing her that His promises were as true as the water dripping into Ishmael's mouth. God's promises to bless His people often look like rivers in the wasteland. In His provision, God may choose to make a path, a road, or a river, but He always provides a way for His people in the dry country.

Whatever desert you may find yourself in, rest assured that God sees you and longs to flood you with hope as you look to Him. Unlike the world's version of hope, our hope is secure and eternal. Our hope does not trust vaguely in well intended, but empty, phrases such as, 'all things happen for a reason,' 'tomorrow is a new day,' or 'keep your chin up and hang in there.' These phrases may be true, but they are shallow and fall short of providing real and lasting hope. As believers, our trust is rooted in the promises of a God, who lavishly provides wells of water in our barrenness; a barrenness that has incredibly redemptive ripple effects. As the ripples spread outward, we can sometimes even see little glimpses of their beauty.

**Reflection:** How awesome that we serve a God Who sees us — really sees us — and offers us a "know-so" hope instead of a "hope-so" hope. Where are you in need of His restoration?

# EMOTIONAL

*This may not be the easiest section to dive into because it may stir up some emotions. It is so important and good to do so in order to be able to love our child(ren) in healthy ways. We need to be equipped to walk with them, and lead them through their own wrestling and journeys. God made us as emotional beings, and He uses our longings to point to what He made us for. Our longings, and our children's longings reveal our absolute need for God. In our need and dependence on Him, He longs for us to have peace in our relationships, as we draw near to those we love.*

## *Better Now Than Later*

**Scripture**: 1 Kings 2, 11, 2 Samuel 7:15-16

**Key idea:** The way you were parented has a direct effect on how you parent. Directly and indirectly, positive and negative traits from our parents will be passed down, unless intervention happens. It is vital that you address and deal with your own emotional issues before you bring your child home. The last thing you want is for your child to be the recipient of your own issues. The first step in dealing with your emotional triggers is to know your own hot buttons. What triggers anxiety or fear in you? What was your childhood attachment style like? What strengths/weaknesses of your parents do you want to model and also avoid? The strengths and weaknesses of our parents play a role in shaping us, however, this does not negate personal responsibility. Regardless of our upbringing, we are able to choose how to harness its influence on us. We see the influence of this trickle -down effect in the father/son relationship of David and Solomon. We see how David's weaknesses affect Solomon, but we also witness David returning to the Lord in repentance, while Solomon (seemingly) did not. David comes before the Lord with a humble, dependent, and repentant heart after his (many) failures. David eventually owns his mistakes and takes personal responsibility. I am so thankful for God's infinite grace, and for His approachability when we mess up! In spite of all of Solomon's unfaithfulness, God still blessed him and remained loyal to His promises to David. That is worth repeating…IN SPITE OF and EVEN THOUGH Solomon turned away… God still stayed near to him. Similarly, even when we turn away in doubt and fear, God promises to draw near to us when we return and draw near to Him. His grace is more than sufficient! Disobedience always has consequences, but even in the consequences, He always gives His children redemption! God knows that we will not be able to leave a perfect example for our children, but we can absolutely leave an influential one. The long-term, eternal gains of dealing with our issues far outweigh our present, short-term sacrifices.

**Reflection:** What is the most pressing personal issue you need to face so that you can embrace your child's issues? If we find hope in an infinitely powerful and loving God, it is possible to be exhausted, yet NOT overwhelmed!

# *Clear As Mud*

**Scripture:** Exodus 34:33-35, 2Corinthians 3:12-18

**Key idea:** God wired us naturally to learn from imitation. Even in our fallen state, God longs for His children to reflect His image. In a similar fashion, your broken and needy child will naturally imitate you. When Moses came down from Mt. Sinai with the writings of the Law, his face physically reflected the fact that he had been speaking directly to God. In Corinthians, Paul explains that as glorious as Moses' face was, it was a fading and temporal glory, because it was outshone by the glory of the Gospel. The Gospel absolutely transforms us into the image of God " from glory to ever increasing glory". As believers, we believe the New Covenant supersedes the old covenant because the veil that obscures our view of God is removed, allowing for our unveiled view. Here, we can behold God's glory, and be transformed into His image. Due to our sin, our view of His image will not become completely unobstructed this side of Heaven; but as we continue to step out of the way, His Spirit continually transforms us into His radiant image.

Practically speaking, what does this mean? First, it means that we will always have relational problems in this fallen, chaotic world. Second, our kids are in the thick of this every day, and they desperately need parents to guide them with the truth. Our hope, in our fallen state, and dealing with fallen people, is found in clinging to God, Who takes pleasure in refining, renewing, and sanctifying us.

**Reflection:** Try this simple but poignant example from the staff of Lifeline Children Services : Take a cup and fill the bottom with some dirt; then add some water; the water will stay relatively clear; but what happens when you place a lid on the water and shake it? It becomes muddy and unclear right? This simple analogy is what happens if we do not deal with our own issues and messes.

Consequently, our child's issues and messes inevitably trigger more of our own, and the water becomes more muddled and compounded for everyone involved.

# *Forward Focused*

**Scripture:** Hebrews 11-12:3, 1 Cor 6:11

**Key ideas:** The importance of being forward focused cannot be understated because the race we run is not a sprint or even a mile, but a marathon. In Hebrews, we are encouraged to active obedience by the many past champions of our faith. In Hebrews 11, Paul encourages his fellow believers as runners in a race, spurred on by a "great cloud of witnesses", the heroes of our faith. These witnesses are not heavenly spectators looking down upon us in approval or disapproval, but they are our models, who have given testimony by their examples. Only by laying aside any hindrances can we put forth our best effort. The sin of unbelief is so crippling in our race of life. In order for us to run our marathon well, we need the Holy Spirit's guidance to run with endurance, persistence, and be forward-focused. His Spirit will be our fuel and our refuel, renewing us more into His likeness. This cycle of forward momentum enables us to not only continue the race, but to continue growing in grace. This process of God perfecting us in holiness is how God sanctifies us, and sanctification is always progressive. This fancy term called progressive sanctification is always forward focused. Our children need us to be forward focused because stuck parents are stagnant, and stagnant parents cannot help their children become unstuck. As growing and trusting believers, God is always making us more and more like Him until we reach our eternal home, where we will finally become like Him.

**Reflection:** Look at the model of faithful "racers" set before us in Hebrews 11, and ask God to refuel and recharge you.

# *Heard By God*

**Scripture:** 1Samuel 1 and Psalm 18

**Key ideas:** No matter what chaos is going on in the world or in our hearts, God hears and sees above the noise. In all the turmoil and materialism of Israel during the period of the judges, Hannah stood out as a woman of faith. Hannah's personal life was one of despair as she wrestled with childlessness and continual badgering from a woman named Peninnah. She pleaded before God with such emotion that the high priest thought she was drunk. Her fervent prayers and tears for a son led her to make a sacred vow unto the Lord. She pleaded with God to put life inside her belly, and pledged to "give it back" to God, if… He would only grant her request. God sees fit to honor her bold and decisive prayer, and He blessed her with Samuel, whose name means "heard by God". She kept her word to the Lord and, at a young age, placed her impressionable son into a defiled worship center. Undoubtedly to many, this act bordered on foolishness, due to the corruption of the times, but it was a pre-arranged sacrifice she made to the Lord. God used her devotion and commitment greatly, granting her the privilege of giving birth to one of the most pivotal judges in Israel's history. After years of wandering, God used Samuel to turn the nation of Israel back to Himself. The Lord hears your heartfelt prayers, just like He heard Hannah's. Yes, He can handle your doubts, fears, even the most twisted of emotions. God always hears, and God always answers, in ways that are best!

**Reflection:** The adoption journey is full of unchartered waters! You are not alone in your journey. God is leading you faithfully and steadily. Do you need to believe the truth that **everything** and **everybody** entrusted to His care is safe in His lavish love?!

# PHYSICAL

*It may seem strange to have a section on physical activity in a book about adoption, but if we start with idea that physical well-being is really a matter of stewardship towards God, and what He has entrusted to us, it makes perfect sense. The goal here is not to turn anyone into an Olympian, but to think holistically in terms of self-care. As a former collegiate athlete and physical trainer of over twenty years, I hope to encourage and challenge you to a healthy self-examination.*

## *Physical Health Is Your Catalyst*

**Scripture:** Psalm 139

**Key idea:** Are there any ways that you can optimize your current health in the areas of fitness, nutrition, and quality sleep? Think about these things in light of the present moment, but also what your life might look like when your child comes home. Think about the times in your day that you have the most, and the least, amounts of energy. Both of these extremes can be great place to start implementing some simple exercise into your day. Yes, finding the time to fit quality exercise, nutrition, and sleep into your day takes some planning and creativity, but once implemented, the positive changes in your outlook and energy level will spur you on.

**Reflection:** Please allow yourself to focus here on a healthy and Biblical mindset, viewing your physical body as God's temple. Begin right where you are, wherever you find yourself on the health and exercise spectrum. You may be starting with the goal of simply increasing your daily steps, or you may have some wonderfully grandiose goals/hopes/plans. Remember that the goal here is to motivate, not produce guilt! Simply, begin where you are. Meditate on Psalm 139 to set your framework.

# *Permissible Is Not Always Beneficial*

**Scripture:** I Corinthians 6:12 and 10:31, Colossians 3:23, Hebrews 4:16

**Key idea:** Some things are just that — permissible, but not helpful or beneficial — to self or others. Maybe there is something you do (habitually or on occasion) that is not inherently sinful, but may not be uplifting to yourself or to another person. In lieu of our Scripture reading, ask God to shed light on any possible thing in your life that is best or helpful. God tells us in Ephesians 1 to be a rare and holy people. What if we approached every decision from a mindset of "what will this decision cost me or someone that I love?" Not a monetary cost but a ripple effect- kind of a cost. We can apply this to every area of our life, but let's stick here with practical physical applications. Think in terms of the basics such as: Am I getting enough sleep? Are my eating choices fueling me or slowing me down? Am I moving enough? These (seemingly) small choices are impactful. There is great wisdom to be gained as we seek to ground every choice we make from the perspective of "what will it cost me or someone I love" perspective. Satan's schemes are often very subtle, as he seeks to lure us into pursuing seemingly good things. We can even pursue good things, but in the wrong way. Or we can even pursue good things, at the wrong time, or with the wrong person.

**Reflection:** Maybe you just need to take a deep breath, and remind yourself that you are perfectly complete in Christ. This belief will give you the freedom to begin right where you are. This belief knows that conviction is from the Lord, but guilt is never from Him. Conviction-yes…but guilt-no! What a gift that we can come before

God's throne with confidence! Armed with His grace and confidence, can you think of any area where you are settling for second best…permissible, but just not helpful?

# *Turn North*

**Scripture :** Daniel 1:8-13 James 1:12-18, 2Corinthians 10:5

**Key idea:** One choice leads to another! This is great news, because this means that any healthy choice we make can (and will) snowball into another good choice. I hope and pray that today's passages inspire you as much as they do me. Daniel models incredible discipline and courage for us. Today, let's focus on whether you think your food choices are fueling you, or hindering you? Don't worry, we are going to stay very simple here, in terms of food. I just want to challenge you to be educated about what and when you eat. Food is a gift to be enjoyed with others, and it's easy to allow the media to leave you overwhelmed and full of questions about whether to follow a low-carb, keto, paleo, vegetarian, Mediterranean, vegan….diet. Exhale and free yourself from the exhaustion of too many options, and simplify. Allow yourself to think in terms of eating food that fuels and energizes. For most people, this will consist of eating a lot of vegetables, fruits, quality proteins, and drinking a lot of water. We know that even the slightest amount of dehydration leaves us feeling sluggish. Excess consumption of simple carbohydrates (pastas, sugars, and breads) often make us incredibly lethargic. At the same time, consumption of complex carbohydrates (vegetables and fruit) and quality proteins (fish, legumes, organic/grass-fed chicken/beef) will, most certainly, ignite us. Think back to our idol devotional…whatever we choose to focus and feed on (literally) will grow. My god(s), both good and bad, have an insatiable hunger. It is no different with God, in the sense that, if we choose to feed on Him, He will grow! It is possible for us to turn our unhealthy food cravings into deeper cravings for God, His Word, and things that honor Him. Pursuing our God-given passions and pursuits that honor Him. He is the only One who can fill us to our core.

**Reflection:** will you allow today's reflection time to make a specific challenge? If so, here it is… can you sneak more veggies/fruit into your day, or possibly cut back on any (brain numbing) starches like bread/sugar? You don't have to do a total revamping here! Really… baby steps!

# *Sustain It!*

**Scripture:** Colossians 2:7 and 1Corinthians 6:19

**Key idea**: God tells us in I Corinthians to take every thought captive in surrender to Him. For most of us, this takes constant re-directing! If you are anything like me, you can experience an amazing reading or prayer time, only to find yourself ten minutes later, battling your sin nature. Thankfully, God not only knows our continual struggle to re-direct our thoughts, but He meets us exactly where we are**.** Re-directing and re-orienting our thoughts require us to go beyond surface change and root deeper into what really matters. For the most part, our behaviors are driven by our thoughts.

We maintain healthy discipline by each NEXT choice we make. Maybe, finding time to exercise is not your challenge, but quality sleep is an issue you want to focus on. Quantity of sleep looks different for everyone, (although most adults function best on at least seven hours) but everyone needs deep quality "REM" sleep in order for cellular repair to take place. Some people thrive on power naps during the day, especially if they are not able to sleep well or long during the night. Just like any other area in life that requires discipline, our physical bodies can sometimes reach a plateau, settling into complacency. A number of factors can cause plateaus: genetics, injury or health issue, hormones, distractibility, lack of prioritizing, life circumstances beyond our control, etc. Even when we are motivated, we can easily hit a lull, especially at the half-way mark. It is here, at the midpoint, the half-time, where we are often in the most need of a fist bump. It is here, where we can find ourselves longing for complacency. It is here that we have a choice to make…the choice to slow down and shrink back, or the choice to dig deep and refocus. So here is my fist bump to you… The time to set/maintain healthy habits is NOW, not when your child comes into your home. I repeat… please don't allow yourself to wallow in self-defeating feelings, just start now! Make the next healthy choice now!

**Reflection:** Are you in need of re-fueling now? Are there any tweaks you can make in your health habits today? Remember that your strength in being a faithful steward comes from small choices and daily self- reminders that God's temple resides in you! Yes, the Spirit of the living God takes His residency in your heart! Sobering and powerful truth! The steeper the hike, the more spectacular the view.

**Extra challenge:** A healthy tomorrow really begins the night before, so what would happen if you went to bed 30 minutes earlier, or woke up 10 mins earlier? What would it look like if you added 5-15 minutes of heart-pumping exercise at the start of your day? Or a set of push-ups and crunches at your mid-afternoon slump? Or possibly, 15 squats or a round of stairs before or after lunch? Could you fit in 10 minutes of jumping jacks, crunches and/or push- ups first thing in the morning? Or perhaps a (guilt-free) afternoon power nap?

# *Sometimes You Just Have To Flee!*

**Scripture:** Genesis 39:1-20 and 1 Corinthians 10:13-14

**Key idea:** Boundaries can actually be freeing! How are you doing at redirecting misguided cravings and patterns of thinking? There is really only One who is capable of satisfying them. As you seek to make healthy life choices, there will always be circumstances or people that have the potential to sway or entice you, intentionally or not, down a path that is not the best. It may be wisest for you to flee from it/them for a season, or even permanently. In MY UTMOST FOR HIS HIGHEST, Oswald Chambers says, "Never let God give you one point of truth which you do not instantly live up to". That is a high calling! This high calling is completely dependent upon His indwelling strength in us. When we run from something, we usually run to something. We want to be a people who run to our Savior when we are tempted. Chambers says that the golden rule in temptation is to go higher. What a great word picture! Growing in grace and character means that we are never stagnant, but that we are always moving towards something or someone.

Maybe there is something you do (habitually or on occasion), that is not inherently sinful, but it's not necessarily uplifting. In lieu of our Scripture reading, ask God to shed light on something in your life that is not helpful or best-even though it may not necessarily be wrong. He calls us to be a rare and holy people. In MY UTMOST FOR HIS HIGHEST, Oswald Chambers says, "Never let God give you one point of truth which you do not instantly live up to". That is a high calling! A calling that is completely dependent upon His indwelling strength in us.

**Reflection:** Is there anybody or anything that has a negative influence on you? Maybe something that not inherently wrong or sinful, but that pulls you away from God, and pulls you toward an idol?

# *Everybody's Got One!*

**Scripture:** 2Corinthians 12:8-10 and Job 42

**Key idea:** We all have at least one! Job had many…Paul had many… Paul however, speaks directly of one in particular. One what? A thorn! Paul repeatedly pleads with God to remove the thorn from his side. There are many theories circulating as to what Paul's thorn was, and although we may not know for sure what his particular thorn was, we do know that God used it mightily to keep Paul humbly dependent on Him. We also know that God uses everything for His glory, and that means e-v-e-r-y-t-h-i-n-g, a-l-w-a-y-s! God even uses evil and satan for His purposes. He allowed satan to take pretty much everything away from Job — for a time. He allowed Paul to have a thorn in his side. The Bible does not tell us if the thorn Paul experienced was physical, emotional, or mental, but we know for sure that it was bothersome to him. God always employs satan to His (God's) own end, to serve Himself and His people. He did it with Job. He did it with Paul. And, God will use it to produce godliness in us also. We just have to do our part in trusting His goodness. God can, and will, use satan to produce godliness in us as we resist the onslaught of our enemy.

Yes, we are to be diligent in praying that the Lord protects us from satan's schemes to tear our families apart, but what if these arrows may be the very things that God uses in our lives to keep us from other sins, e.g. pride and self-reliance. What if the very thing that we are asking God to take away is the very thing that God wants to use — right now — as His greatest gift? Job reached a state of mourning that I cannot imagine, but ended up praising God. After a season of confusion and much loss, Job clearly humbled himself before God. God graciously saw fit to give Job "twice as much as he had before" (Job 42:10). Similarly, Paul prayed fervently for the Lord to take his thorn away, but he also eventually gave thanks for it, and regarded it as a help rather than a handicap. The thorn became the place where Paul, who wrote more on grace than anyone else, needed much grace. Paul understood that even personal victories and strengths can be barriers in our experiencing God's grace. What does this mean for us? We can be sure that God knows, sees, and uses the redemptive power of thorns in our lives. Chip Ingram says, "God always brings about the best possible end, by the best possible means, for the most possible people, for the longest possible time; so, if there was a kinder, gentler, or easier way for His will to be worked out, then He would have us experience it that way". God is always good, and He always loving, and He always uses our life experiences to conform us more into His image.

**Reflection:** Are you wrestling with any thorns? Remind yourself that if God has allowed it, He has not left the throne, and He will absolutely use it. Nothing is ever wasted, and God will use it for your good and His glory. Pray for the strength to endure — even embrace — the thorns He is allowing, even if you cannot fully understand why.

# MARRIAGE

*It is SO important to stay united as one as we seek to parent and love our child(ren). One thing we know for sure, is that adoption will challenge your marriage greatly. That being said, our marriages can thrive under the challenges, but this will take much intentionality. Prayerfully read Philippians 2 and James 5:16 (together if possible), and give yourself, and your spouse, the freedom to be honest about your relational challenges. Temper your honesty with humility, and you will be ready to dive into our marriage section.*

# *The Litmus Test*

**Scripture:** Ephesians 4:1-3, Galatians 5:13, Matthew 19:5-6

**Key idea:** The genuine test of our love is the ability to self-sacrifice. Christ gave up His rightful position in heaven to sacrifice for us in the greatest way imaginable! In His time on earth, He showed us what sacrificial love looks like. The one Who should have been served, chose to serve. Because marital love is esteemed above all other earthy loves, it is one of the best places to practice living for the sake of Christ. Our deepest need, and our greatest joy, is found more in **giving** love, than on receiving love. We are told in Ephesians to live worthy of our calling by being humble, patient, and gentle with one another, and we would be remiss if we didn't carry this over to our marriage. in his book *Sacred Parenting*, Gary Thomas says it well.: "In marriage, we have been enlisted in the most glorious work ever known: the advancement of God's kingdom; and in creating a marriage worthy of this calling means that we create a marriage where the character of Christ is displayed for all to see. " Convicting, huh?! Ephesians was written to a culture (like ours today) that did not really value humility. We are called to model the servanthood of Christ.

This completely changes our marital motivations from ones that seek to build ourselves up, into ones that portray Jesus- to our spouse, and also to the world. God gives us grace after grace for our continual mess-ups. Our spouse needs us to extend the same grace that we have been given. Extending grace and making allowances for their mess-ups is ineffective on our own. We are able to extend grace BECAUSE OF the grace given to us, and because of His power that flows in and through us. Naturally (and hopefully), we will experience happiness in our marriages, but God primarily seeks our holiness. God reconciled us to Himself so that we can be reconciled with each other. We have an amazing opportunity to show the love and servanthood of Christ to those around us in the way we treat and love our spouse.

**Reflection:** How can you be more gentle and humble today with your spouse? Putting it in writing might serve as a helpful reminder for those "extra-grace needed" weary days! Is there somewhere that you can make an allowance instead of a judgement? God sees our heart and knows when our motives are pure. Pray for pure motives as you seek to be united in love with your spouse.

# *Small Fractures Lead To Big Cracks*

**Scripture:** Ephesians 4:29-32

**Key idea:** People who have been married for a while will attest to the fact that marriages go through many different stages. These stages will change and evolve as circumstances change. This is especially true when you bring your child home. Your marriage will be different indefinitely, and this is okay!

Strong marriages require intentionality from both partners in order to be able to ebb and flow with the life changes.

Even the strongest of marriages have the potential to crack under new pressure. Lifeline has worked with literally thousands of adoptive couples, and they stress the importance of couples dealing proactively with potential conflicts. Dealing with the (seemingly) little things is so important, because research shows that marriages with only small hairline fractures can end up with canyons separating them if proper preparations and repairs are not made.

We each come into marriage bringing not just our own history, but all of our family's history as well. Some of this generational baggage may even be outside of our own awareness. It is imperative that children see their parents respecting each other. Truly, the best way for parents to love their kids is by loving each other well. Kids need to see their parents living out their love for each other-right before their eyes. We know that little things lead to big things, and the little things- if left unchecked-will lead to even bigger things. Sarcasm is a perfect example of a "little" thing that can harden the heart of one spouse to another. Although sometimes funny and innocent, it can often be damaging. Let's be honest, we don't always "feel" like loving our spouse- right?! Sometimes we have to act lovingly even if we do not feel the love. Even our adult- brains are still being "rewired" as we allow God to soften and smooth the little marital cracks.

You will naturally be spending a lot of time bonding with your adopted child (a good and necessary thing), and time with your spouse will probably be more quality than quantity. Thus, the importance of dealing with the little cracks cannot be understated.

**Reflection:** Is there an area of your marriage that is not blossoming? If so, will you commit to giving it your complete attention to make it bloom? Don't let the little cracks lead to gaping canyons. Awareness is the first step…awareness leads to conviction…conviction leads to repentance…and repentance leads to change. Small steps… baby steps….

# "Fix Or "Fit"

**Scripture:** Ephesians 5:22-33, 1Thessalonians 5:11

**Key idea:** We are all at different places in our marriage journeys. Although ineffective (and not very healthy), it is natural to look to our spouse to fix or fit something inside of us. Consciously or unconsciously, we might hope for them to fix a particular sin pattern, a faulty pattern of relating that we have developed. We may even long for them to fix or heal our hurtful past. Whatever it may be, we will always be discouraged when we hold them responsible for "fixing" us. On the other hand, we might try to conform them to fit into a certain personality type, or into a way of relating that suits our needs. This unhealthy pattern of relating, is often due to past choices and relationships. It is easy to default to what is comfortable and familiar, even if these patterns have proven to be self- defeating.

In a perfect world, our reactions to our spouse would perfectly model the patterns set before us in Scripture… but, in our fallen world and sinful nature…we (typically) instinctively respond from our own sin and woundedness. Only through the indwelling Holy Spirit can we lovingly respond to each other in grace and truth.

The marriage relationship, even in its imperfection, can and will, set the tone in our homes. Marriage is intended to depict the Gospel, and our interactions will absolutely look different when we model our relational God. This relational God is always pursuing our hearts and showing us how to "do" relationships better. His beautiful plan for marriage is for us to experience His view of the Trinity here on earth: God, husbands, and wives. Within our marriage, we shape and refine each other as we let go and let God do His work of relational healing in our hearts.

**Reflection:** If marriage truly sets the tone of love (or lack of) in your home, think about the way you respond/react to your spouse. Are you responding to your spouse in the way that you want to respond to your children? I am humbled as I ask myself this same question. Write down a few simple ways that you can encourage your spouse?

# *A Devoted "I Will Go" Love*

**Scripture:** Genesis 24 and Ruth 1

**Key idea**: You will probably want to read and catch the details of Genesis 24 and Ruth 1 before reading this entry. For the sake of time, we will focus on Rebekah's story from our Genesis passage, but please re-read the story of Ruth. Abraham gave his servant what probably seemed like an insurmountable task. It is safe to say that this was definitely not a conventional way of finding a spouse! Yes, times and customs were different back then, but even this story is a romance that only God could ordain. Abraham charged his servant with these bold words that he had received from the Lord: "The Lord before whom I have walked, will send His angel with you and make your journey a success" (Genesis 24: 40).He did not waste any time as he responded in immediate faith and set out on a journey to find a noble wife for his son Isaac, Rebekah (and her family),

This passage inspired me to look up synonyms for "devoted". The words "loyal, faithful, true, steadfast, constant, committed convinced, dedicated, devout" all followed. We see many examples of devoted love in the Bible, and we see it clearly demonstrated in the words of Rebekah and Ruth. The simple but profound words, "I will go". They uttered these words, and immediately their actions followed. They gave up literally everything for the sake of love (Rebekah to Isaac and Ruth to Naomi). We marvel at the way the Lord lovingly orchestrated the events of Abraham's life in bringing his servant to find a faithful wife for his son Isaac. Abraham's servant had just seen God's hand, and he was anxious to return home and tell his master everything. Rebekah had just met this man who claimed that God had led him to her to propose marriage for his master Isaac. We have to wonder…did she sense that God was in it, orchestrating this moment for her… or did she step out in a trembling, but bold faith? Whatever her feelings, her faith is astounding! Her willingness to go with this man, this stranger, that she met by a stream. Her seemingly simple, but life-changing words "I will go" exemplified a much grander story, one that she (most-likely) never imagined! As those simple words formed on her lips, the camels were readied, and her family sent her off with this prophetic "stranger".

**Reflection:** Most people's story does not seem as romantic as Ruth's or Rebekah's, but as God's special children, all of our stories are unique and divinely orchestrated. Your marriage, your circumstances, your waiting time, every single detail…is all part of the Master Painter's handiwork. He has orchestrated the beginning, the middle, and the ending for you. May the God of grace give us more faith to say "I will go" and "I will follow His lead in every aspect of our marriage and life!

# *Really What It's All About...*

**Scripture:** Genesis 2:18-24 and John 13:35 and 17:23

**Key idea**: In his podcast, Paul Tripp eloquently states that "A solid and lasting relationship of unity is not rooted in relational skill, but it's rooted in worship." He insightfully talks about worship being at the center of everything we say and do, because we are always worshipping something or someone. The first time I heard him say this- that we are always worshipping someone or something-it really stretched my thinking. If this thinking is true, it naturally brings a sense of purpose and intentionality to absolutely everything we do. Apply this to our marriages, this means that loving our spouse well translates to loving Jesus well, while a failure to love our spouse, (enough) is really a failure to love God (enough). Tripp expands on this idea that If we want to love our spouses with the love of Jesus, it is imperative that we always seek to love vertically before we can ever expect to be able to love horizontally. In this way, worship becomes more of an "identity than merely an activity".

Let's be honest, in our flesh, we often want the best possible result with the least amount of effort. Even though our love for our spouse runs deep, we are flawed and selfish in our core. Marriage is not a 50-50 thing! When I remind myself that by loving my spouse well, I am, in reality, really loving Jesus well. Maybe this means that I don't even think about percentages at all. Marriage can survive, but not thrive unless we are willing to go all in.

**Reflection:** If you put Jesus's face in the place of your spouse, how would that change the way you love and respond to your mate? Pray for grace to see your spouse through the lens of Jesus today. This could be a game changer!

# *YOUR ADOPTED CHILD*

# *Huge Mosaic Of Redemption*

**Scripture:** James 1:27, Psalm 8:4-5

**Key idea:** Loving others in general can be messy, but choosing to pursue and love a child who has known loss and trauma will stir up a lot inside of us. This emotional stirring will appear in different forms and through various seasons of our lives and parenting. It is essential to keep connecting back to the Truth, reminding and refreshing ourselves that we have been pursued by God, and that is our basis for pursuing our children. We love… simply because… we have been shown love. Adoption is beautiful and redemptive because it is a response to our Father's love for us, but it is also messy because it started with loss.

With the privilege of adoption and caring for one another with the hands and feet of Jesus, we always need to be mindful of the way we view our role as parents. It can be tempting to fall into the false mind-set that we are somehow "saving" our child. Other people tell us how "amazing" we are for going to such great lengths to "rescue" an orphaned child, and we might (consciously or unconsciously) attempt to take on this "savior" or "rescuer" role or mentality towards our child. Although understandable, let's be clear — we are not our child's rescuer or savior. Yes, adoptive children are most likely leaving a hard place to go to a better, more loving place/home, but there is still an undercurrent of loss for them. Even if they're life has been extremely hard, it was still the life that they knew, and there is a comfort in this.

What a privilege to be a tool in the hands of God, helping to bring some form of beauty from their loss — just like Jesus does for us. Jennifer Phillips, in her book 30 DAYS OF HOPE says it this way, we are honored that the Lord would "love us enough to turn our world upside down and give us greater compassion and depths of love we did not know possible." Her beautiful prayer says it all, "God, who am I that You would love me enough, call me, as imperfect and sinful as I am, to parent this one who is so dearly loved by You? To strip me of deeply rooted idols of security and ease, enlarge my view of the world, and gift me with compassion for the least of these?"

Our privileged role is to shepherd our children and guide them to their Redeemer. Their lives have undoubtedly been rough around the edges, but when viewed in light of God's huge mosaic of redemption, they will definitely not be discounted. God will mightily use their hardships and their blessings as He links His unique mosaic — IN and THROUGH them! As your child grows to trust Christ, He will use them mightily *because of,* not, *in spite* of, their past.


**Reflection:** How has your personal redemption story shaped your view of adoption? How do you view your role in responding to James 1:27?

# *A Unique Path*

**Scripture:** Isaiah 41:13 and 43:19; 2Corinthians 5:17 and 10:5

**Key idea**: Although it may seem obvious, it is important to remember that there is really no such thing as a "healthy" child that has been institutionalized, and your parenting will reflect this truth. Parenting will look different for children that have experienced loss and abandonment. Because of this, your parenting methods will likely cause (well meaning) family and friends to question your methods and actions. Expect this, so that you are not caught off guard when this happens. We will talk about this more in the next section, "Did she really just say that," but for now allow yourself to rest confidently in the fact that parenting a child from hard place will look different.

Thankfully, God is in the renewal business. When we let go and allow Him to work, He always works to renew, restore, and even re-make all of us. It is so hard for a parent to see their child struggling in any capacity, but we have to remember that God uses ALL things for His glory as we trust Him. Pray through every experience and emotion, and pray for your child to see and experience God's comfort, provision, and presence in every situation… past and present. You will likely not know all the details of their past hurts, but your faithful and reliable presence will serve as a comfort.

Your child's experiences have shaped their view of the world, the people in it, and even God. Your child's life has been anything but typical, and remind yourself of the great privilege that God has given you to uniquely parent. Pray for wisdom, as you inhale and exhale God's peace and strength. The bonding between you may be quicker than expected or it may take years, but it will come- as a result of your consistent love. You (and your family) are probably the most consistent presence that your child has ever known. Yes, their past is an ingredient of the present, but it is not an indicator for the future.

**Reflection:** Learn, memorize, and preach this timeless truth to yourself: MY CHILD'S BEHAVIOR IS NOT ABOUT ME!!

# *Why The Anger?*

**Scripture:** Galatians 6:9-10, Psalm 34

**Key idea:** Don't let the reality that your adopted child will deal with some sort of sadness and/or anger allow you to doubt your calling. Our Scripture reading for today encourages us to seek God when we are physically, mentally, and emotionally tired. As parents, we will undoubtedly know what it's like to be tired. Being tired however, does not have to equate with being weary and overwhelmed.

The waiting time is a good time to think through strategies for the potential heated moments. Begin by reminding yourself that simply being present with your child will build trust. Little things, such as verbal praise, eye contact, laughter, and appropriate touch go a long way. Anger, sadness, and grief will look and manifest differently for each child. In spite of the fact that your child is excited to be a part of your family, he/she will also be filled with many mixed emotions. It is also important for you to expect your child to be sad as he leaves behind all that is familiar. Even if their past was heartbreaking, it was all that he/she has ever known, and that in itself, is a source of comfort. Grief and sadness can show up in your child through a host of acting-out behaviors, but common ones are apathy, control issues, and excessive independence or dependence. The fact that your child can grieve and express their grief in all its forms (sadness, anger, anxiety, etc) is actually because they are in a safe place to do so.

Give yourself grace, knowing that you will not always say the right thing-or even know what to say, and you may even respond negatively to your child. If you do respond inappropriately, humbly acknowledge it to your child, and they will hopefully be able to one day mirror your example. Remember, authenticity breads authenticity. The more we use proactive strategies with our child, the less we will have to use reactive strategies. A child coming from a hard place has a broken wing that needs grace, understanding, teaching, correcting, mentoring, and modeling from you. Remember what you preached to yourself yesterday! Over time, you will be able to implement some different training techniques such as redirecting, giving choices, and offering "re-do's". Implementing these techniques early on will set the stage for future success.

They need to see that you are not going anywhere, and that you love them-even in their angry and sad moments. They have probably never had an adult stick around and teach them how to deal with their conflicting emotions. Be prepared for them to take their anger out on you because they have no idea how to process their wounds. The more grounded you are in God's Truth, and the more you understand that your child is acting/reacting the only way they currently know how to, the less you will take their words and woundedness personally. Expect to be challenged, even rejected, while your kids are adjusting to their new life. It is normal and healthy for them to grieve the life that they left behind. Even if it was a sad life, it was the only life they knew.

**Reflection:** How do you need to step back to adjust your expectations!

# *Tiny Seeds*

**Scripture:** Ephesians 1:15-22 and John 17:24-26

**Key idea:** Think of your child as being like a tiny little seed waiting to burst out and bloom. The seeds are dormant until they are given love and nourishment. Dr. Karyn Purvis, author of The Connected Child, goes into great detail about this. (Side-note: If you have not read her book, I cannot recommend it enough! Her book and website offer a variety of support, videos, etc. to parent children from hard places.) She goes into eloquent detail as she compares the childhood brain to plastic. Neurologically, it takes about 400 connections to change a learned pathway. For the child who has experienced trauma, harsh words spoken to them will actually build more reactionary fibers in their brain. While this may sound daunting, the reverse cycle is also true. Research shows that calming words will also grow and cycle into new fiber pathways. As parents, we have this amazing privilege to nurture and grow these little seeds that have graciously been entrusted to us. The fact that that our child's brain can actually be ruptured, means that it can also be repaired. Purvis says it this way: "They can learn to adapt and get back online and then can actually be inspired to rewire". With time, devotion, and a lot of prayer, these precious buds will blossom. As parents, we do not...and cannot...force them to grow, but we can lovingly provide a foundational superstructure, as we water and nurture our little seeds. In the same way that seeds cannot grow without proper nourishment, light, and water, spiritual growth cannot occur outside of relationships. Spiritual growth is progressive, and it can only occur where life is actually being lived in fellowship with others, rooted and founded on Christ as the foundational superstructure.

**Reflection:** Thank God for the opportunity He has given you to help plant and nurture a precious seed! Praise Him for the joy and privilege in being a gardener that helps your child blossom and bloom!

# *Yes, This Is Normal!*

**Scripture:** Romans 2:4, Hebrews 10:14, Lamentations 3:23, Ephesians 2:5

**Key idea:** Growth is really hard to measure! So hard, in fact, that we sometimes do not see it happening in us...or in our children. I want to encourage you here! If we are relying on Christ — really trusting Him — we are guaranteed growth. We are guaranteed growth because of that big word sanctification.' Hebrews 10:14 says, "Christ has completely cleansed and perfected those who have been made holy." Christ has already done the sacrificial, substitutionary work, and we are the blessed beneficiaries. Our status is deemed holy. This status does not mean that we have already achieved holiness, but that as Christ followers, He is working in us and making us new every day. Every day! In this life, we will always wrestle with our flesh, but growth is happening. As we "grow" smaller and God becomes larger.

You may find yourself asking the question, "is this normal for my child to act this way?" This question is relative to the individual and worth exploring to see if professional counseling is needed, but the point here is to expect post-adoption difficulties! Issues with transitions, sleep, food, grief, bonding, relationships, etc. are "normal"! Your consistent love will do wonders in their healing process — and, it will be a process. Focus on picking your battles, and focus on one or two things at a time. Remember, God doesn't refine us all at one time...He does it slowly... with patience. We never want to force or push our children to talk about their past hurts. Temper your responses, especially if you are feeling shocked or overwhelmed on the inside. Sometimes your child just needs to be heard and reminded that their relationship with you is a bond that can never be broken. Although tempting, try not to over-analyze and play the detective role too much. Truly, we may never know if our child's anger, sadness, and/or indifference, is a result of past hurt/trauma, or if it is just plain old sin. Our role is to meet our child with grace and truth... right where they are. We are all on a mission from the Lord, to exemplify God's eternal love to our children, encouraging them with His Truths.

**Reflection:** Remind yourself that attachment does not come over night. It is okay not to feel connected to your child instantaneously because this process takes time. You may sometimes feel more like a mentor than a parent, and that is also okay! Talk through this with your spouse, taking it ultimately to the Lord in prayer. Praise Him for His deliverance, that not only frees us from the penalty of sin, but also frees us (and our children) from the POWER of sin in us!

# YOUR CURRENT FAMILY

*This section is addressed to families that already have children in the home. If this does not apply to you, feel free to focus in on the other sections.*

# High Investment Now=High Return Later

**Scripture:** Ecclesiastes 3:1-8

**Key idea:** We would be remiss if we focused solely on caring for our adopted child, without first addressing our current household. Our family has also been called to this adoption journey, and they are here with us on the front lines. Their support and investment are an essential component on our journey together of bringing our child home. Your children are probably excited about welcoming another child into your home, but there will be moments (when your adoption is finalized) that their sense of normal daily life will be disrupted for the sake of your new child. Schedules will look different, and time spent together will naturally be adjusted. Selfishness will be exposed as each of you makes sacrifices for the good of one another. This continual process of learning to deny self for the sake of another is so hard as it exposes so much, but it can also be beautiful and redemptive. In the same way that you preach self-denial to yourself, you will probably have to coach your children through some jealousy, as everyone is learning how to share and give of their time and energy. Prior to bringing your child home, see if you can involve your kids in the journey as much as possible. Find the balance of involving them in decisions (such as room decor, fundraising ideas/actions, language-learning (if adopting internationally), and, most importantly, in praying together.

Before you bring your "new" child home, your current investment in spending as much quality time with your children as you can, is invaluable. Let them express their excitement, as well as their concerns. They need to know that your love for them is strong and unchanging, even though it will look differently when you bring your new child home. Initially (and indefinitely), your adopted child will need more of your time and energy due to a number of needs, but it will be exciting to see your kids step up, and become leaders for their new sibling (s). The main thing for now is to just take advantage of this waiting time, and spend quality time together.

**Reflection:** Where can you spend more T I M E with your child doing something that he/she loves. Even if it's something you have no interest in-your child will sense this and it will mean even more. Be sure to let them choose the activity, and then go do it together!

# *Pride Can Be Subtle*

**Scripture:** Matthew 18:12, 2Corinthians 11:25, Acts 5:1-11

**Key idea**: If someone asked you, "what are you most proud of" or "what is your greatest achievement" what would you say? It is possible to be outwardly humble, but inwardly boasting and living by our own perceived merits. We can even boast in the busyness of the good "work" of adoption. I'm sure we have all received some form of a pat on the back, when a friend or family member says something like "I could never do what you are doing" or "you are such a good person for adopting," or shares a similar sentiment. Because adoption is self-sacrificing, it is enticing to fall into the false belief that adoption merits some kind of a badge of honor. Intentional or not, we can so easily make our adoption about us. In the same way that our motives for adoption can be misunderstood, we may need to "remind" ourselves that the reason we are pursuing adoption is the SAME reason that we have been pursued by God from the beginning of time. Jesus came to earth and showed us how to live a completely selfless, Christ, and others-centered life. At the center of His teaching is the foundational belief that it is far better to give than to receive. We will always wrestle with our selfish desires, but in our wrestling, we also see that He faithfully comes near to, and rescues the humble in heart. Look no farther than the shepherd who left his ninety-nine sheep for the pursuit and rescue of one. Our mission in adoption is seeking out the one lost sheep in response to God's relentless pursuit of us.

We can also look to Paul, who had many reasons to boast, but rested in the power of Christ alone. Paul experienced unimaginable beatings, stonings, shipwrecks, imprisonments, hunger, and sleeplessness for the sake of the kingdom, but he kept his eyes fixed on his mission. On the flip side of humility, we see how seriously God takes the sin of false pride in the story of Ananias and Saphira. They were even performing noble deeds, but they went too far in trying to appear more spiritual than they really were. Their story causes me to shudder!

**Reflection:** Lord, cleanse us of pride-subtle and blatant. Cleanse us Father, of this fundamental attitude deep within all us that underlies all sin.

# *Did She Really Say That?!*

**Scripture** : 1Thessalonians 5:15 and Ephesians 4:2

**Key idea:** Adoptive families could fill a book with "helpful, well-meaning" phrases from friends and family. How do we show grace to our family members when they speak insensitive and intrusive words? We probably all have someone in our life that has that special gift of irritating us, and successfully knows how to push all of our buttons! We can get ahead of some of the heartache if we assume that their comments or questions are said with our best interests in mind. Even if their words are (deliberately) hurtful, it always makes for a wonderful opportunity to share what God's miracle of adoption really means. We can take their words to the Lord, and pray deliberately and reflectively for them. Take your mother in law, for example, (shot in the dark here) who probably means well, but needs to be educated on how parenting a child from a hard place looks differently. Remember the questions that you had before you began, and it will be easier to extend grace. Try not to become so consumed with preparing yourself and your immediate family, that you neglect to share your knowledge with others in your extended family. Humbly assume that they have your best interests in mind. Assume that they come to the table with limited knowledge. This mindset will help you to feel and extend grace. If you choose to share pertinent information so that they might understand your decisions, know that they might not embrace your views and passions. This will be also be helpful when your child comes home. If-and when-your feelings get trampled on, try to take a step back, even laugh it off if you feel so inclined, and direct your attention to the Divine Director in charge of the entire show. These moments are golden opportunities. They provide the chance to educate others about the plight of orphans, and the story of our own spiritual adoption. Maybe they have never thought about the fact that we all share this "orphaned child" status-before God rescued us.

**Reflection:** Pray for the grace to respond and take to the Cross every word (past, present, and future) spoken to you. Disclaimer alert: You will probably do this repeatedly in this (adoption) life that you have embraced. It only takes a split- second decision to decide that you will respond -and not react- before you speak. God hears our spoken and unspoken prayers, so why not take your response to the cross before you take it out on someone else?!

# *Always Upside Down*

**Scripture:** Philippians 2:3-11, Matthew 23:11-12, John 13:13-15

**Key idea:** Our Lord and Savior, King of Kings and Lord of Lords, willingly chose a life of servanthood. He chose a bed of straw over a dignified palace, and a lineage of poverty versus royalty. He chose to spend His limited time on this earth serving those who were not esteemed and valued, according to this world's standards. Our Lord, Who WILLINGLY left the crown of Heaven for a life of selfless devotion and suffering, always flips our ideas upside down. He taught with words of life, and demonstrated His words with a life of foot washing service. He tells us that in order to become great, we must become the lowest. To become first, we must become last. In a world where everything revolves around self-protection, self-comfort, self-promotion, and self-preservation, Jesus calls us to deny ourselves. He wants us to live in this upside down, counter cultural manner.

Humanly speaking, Paul (after his conversion) is a wonderful model of living life in this upside-down servanthood. He claims that although he has nothing, he possesses everything. Now that is an upside-down mentality that will enable us to push our pride aside as we serve others!

**Reflection:** Take some time to praise our humble Servant-King. How are you inspired to serve someone, and live life upside down-for the sake of the Gospel?

# *Freed For A Purpose*

**Scripture:** Romans 5:9-11 and 6:15-23; Galatians 5:13-14!

**Key idea:** Christ freed us from sin's bondage for real purposes! In the previous devotional, we talked about how God is always flipping our ideas upside down. Today, we take that even deeper, as we get to see a small glimpse of Christ pursuing our freedom- through calling us to become His slaves. The term slave does not usually equate with the way we think about freedom, does it? The world might define freedom as being able to act any way you choose, but is this really freedom? It might sound good on the surface, but this kind of freedom is really a subtle form of bondage! Because we are His children, we are completely redeemed (saved) and completely justified (in right standing with God through Jesus' payment). His redemption purchased our freedom, and blessed us with many incredible privileges, titles, and identities. Who would have known that one of the most privileged identity is that of being called a slave…His esteemed slave?! Call it a royal slave, because it's the best kind of slave there is…a delivered and liberated one! Our deliverance is a two- fold deliverance "from": a deliverance from the consequences of sin and death; and a deliverance from the power of sin over us. Not only are we set free from death and its enslaving power for the future, but we are set free from whatever is weighing us down right now. Our sin may temporarily be enslaving or binding, but it does not define us. As children and slaves, we are personally bound to the One Who has all power and authority! Being free for a purpose means being a "willing" slave to righteousness, because a freedom to act any way we choose is not freedom at all!

**Reflection:** Knowing and rejoicing that we are free from the judgment of self and others, compels us in our freedom for service to Him and others! Is there anything that you would like to be free of right now?

# OTHER PEOPLE

*So far, we have discussed our relationships in terms of those immediate to us: God, self, spouse, family, our future children. This last section, "Others", is one I might have left out prior to our adoption, but when I think holistically, it is relevant. It is relevant because Christ calls us to be "salt and light" to the world around us. Let's dive in!*

# Cul-De-Sac Christianity

**Scripture**: Ephesians 1:15-2:10, Matthew 5:13-14, Hebrews 13:21

**Key idea:** In our very first devotional, we set our entire foundation for pursuing our child. The driving factor for pursuit is the reality that as a child, Christ first pursued us. This was not a "won and done" kind of pursuit! Out of His perfect and unmerited love, God rescued us, and continues to rescue us, His children. This continued awareness can powerfully pry open our eyes and hearts, uprooting the cobwebs of pride, criticism, and complacency. This uprooting, by the power of the Holy Spirit, allows us to fully embrace His love so that we overflow with His love to others. We can only give away what we already possess. When the cobwebs build up, our view of self becomes too big, and our view of God becomes wayyy too small, leaving our ability to give Gods love drastically diminished. If given away at all, it may be limited in its scope so that only those in our "cul-de-sac" are the recipients. It's easy to lose sight of the fact that the Gospels scope goes well beyond our families and cul-de-sacs. It's so easy to grow complacent while we are waiting! We are sent to advance the Gospel, even in our waiting weariness, to give ourselves away for the cause His kingdom. We are sent outward, and we get to join in the mission of Christ; He tells us, "as the Father has sent me, so I send you." We don't have to be weary, because what He calls us to do, He equips us to do! He calls us to be the "salt and light" in this world.

**Reflection:** It is easy to become so fixated on the process of adoption, that we might miss opportunities to advance His gospel? Join me in prayer, that our view of self will become smaller, as our view of God grows exponentially.

# *Who Are You Listening To?*

**Scripture:** Nehemiah 6, Hebrews 4:16, James 3:13-18

**Key idea:** What voice is on autopilot in your head? God calls us to run to Him, so that we hear His voice when our fear-based thinking starts to creep in. The importance of speaking truth to ourselves cannot be overstated. We can get overwhelmed with other peoples' ideas, or even, what we convince ourselves that other people are thinking. If we were to get in the thoughts of others, we might be surprised that they are not even thinking of us at all! Instead of listening to our own inner critic, and that of others, perhaps we just need to listen (to self and others) less, and self-talk (the Gospel truths) more. In other words, preaching the Gospel to self probably involves listening to self …less!

Nehemiah is a great example of someone who could have easily given in to fear, if he allowed the defeating thoughts (of self and others) to deter him. Instead, he chose to let God's voice be His replay button. He set his face like flint on God's plan. Similarly, God is calling you to set your face like flint to what He is calling you to do right now- at this moment. God's power in you is more than sufficient. He will impart to you strength beyond measure, so that all you need… is all that you have… and all that you have…is more than enough

**Reflection:** What voice is on autopilot in your mind? Is it a voice of truth? If you are a music lover, Casting Crowns has a great song called "The Voice of Truth" if you want to check out.

I heard one time that we are, to a certain degree, the sum of the five people we spend the most time with. If this is even half true, the importance of surrounding yourself with people who encourage you to make Godly choices is fundamental to hearing His voice.

# *Triumphal Parade*

**Scripture:** 2Corinthians 2:14-17 , Ephesians 5:1-2 and Proverbs 3:3-4

**Key idea:** The very fact that we have been "commissioned" by Christ, assures us that we are being led forward into victory! This victory is a sure thing for the sole reason that God is the Initiator and the Leader. Since He is the One who has given us the privilege and responsibility of parenthood, He is One in charge of commission. Our commission is for His Name sake, and He assures us that if He calls us to a task, He will see it through. Paul uses the image of a triumphal parade in the Corinthian passage from today's reading. Paul, formerly an enemy of God, was now taken "captive" by Christ and led in triumph.

Following battle victories, the Romans burned incense in parades, and Paul was comparing this aroma with the sweet-smelling fragrance diffused by those whom Christ has captured with His love. Thankfully, we no longer have to sacrifice animals since Christ became our ultimate sacrifice, but God desires His people to offer a fragrant sacrifice to Him- through living the holy lives. This aroma is not only sweet to God, but also sweet to our fellow believers. Our journey God has given us comes with great privileges, duties, and responsibilities. As we let Him take His rightful place as our Leader, He will guide our every step, ensuring that we march in triumph through every trial!

**Reflection:** Ask our great Commissioner to give you renewed strength and courage for your mission. Who needs to be a part of your sweet- smelling aroma today? Close today by praying boldly for every single person involved in your adoption journey. Every person…family members, social workers, government workers, court officials, and any one of the blessed souls that will play a role in your adoption. Proverbs 3:3-4 says: Never let loyalty and kindness leave you! Tie them around your neck as a reminder. Write them deep within your heart. Then you will find favor with both God and people, and you will earn a good reputation.

# *A Fragrant Life*

**Scripture:** Acts 12:5-17

**Key idea**: Her name was Rhoda. Maybe you have heard of her? She is in the book of Acts, but prior preparing this study on living a fragrant life, I had honestly never given her a second thought. After a closer study of the book of Acts, I am only intrigued, inspired, and humored by her! Rhoda, whose name means "rose", was an ordinary household servant with an extra-ordinary faith. Here is the setting:

A group was gathered late one night for prayer in the home of (John Mark's mother) Mary. James (the brother of John) had recently been put to death for his faith, and the people feared that Peter might be next. The Bible footnotes that the group was praying late one night for the release of Peter from prison, when Rhoda heard a knock at the door. She ran to the door, and immediately recognized Peter's voice. What follows makes me laugh out loud, as well as feel an immediate kindred spirit with Rhoda! Rhoda, in her excitement, failed to open the door to let Peter in, and left Peter standing OUTSIDE the closed gate. She then darted into the room where everyone was praying, and announced that Peter himself was standing at the door. Not only did they not believe her, but they questioned her sanity. Remember… they were praying for Peter's release at the time of his appearance! Apparently, it was a common Jewish belief that every Israelite was given a guardian angel- who actually looked like him. Rhoda, even in her excitement, never doubted that it was Peter! She saw Peter's face, and she experienced the joy of being able to participate in kingdom work. Her job as a household-servant might have been mundane, but her faith was anything but mundane!

**Reflection:** Living a fragrant life does not have to mean that we have a high-power job! It does mean that we live by a Higher Power in genuine, bold, and believing faith!

# *In Closing*

It is my hope and prayer that the Lord has, and will continue, to use this book to draw you deeper into His love, power, and presence. But don't stop there! I pray that you will take His great love and power to hurting and hungry souls.

God's love is the greatest life-altering truth that we will ever know. Waiting for something that we want is never easy, but God is always working. He is never dormant, but He is constantly working- in and through us- as we wait. Be assured that you are not alone, and many flawed yet faithful ones have paved the way before you. Know also that I am praying for you and your family. Even if we have never met, this book was written with you in mind. May this be just the beginning of your beautiful life-long endeavor of basking in our Heavenly Father's amazing grace.

# *A Note From The Author*

Missy Grant, wife, mom, and author of the book Trails for Ticos "stumbled upon" a love of writing in her passionate response to the Lord's heart for adoption. > Missy and her husband adopted two children from Costa Rica through Lifeline Children Services. The plight of the millions of orphans around the world opened her eyes and changed her life. She continues to advocate for vulnerable children and their families. Missy also works as a Pilates and fitness trainer. When she is not spending time with her family, she can likely be found mountain biking or running trails with their dog, Reo. She loves escaping to the beach for countless hours of surfing and family fun!

Sometimes, taking the first step is the most challenging. Sometimes, it is the waiting. Press on, dear friends, in the depth and breadth and height of his unquenchable love! I would love to connect with you!

**Follow Me on:**

Instagram at Missygrant49
Facebook (Missy Grant)
Missygrant49@gmail.com

# Sources and Quotes

*My Utmost for His Highest* by Oswald Chambers, Discovery House Publishers, Grand Rapids, 1994.

*30 Days of Hope for Adoptive Families* by Jennifer Phillips New Hope Publishers.com 2017

*Sacred Parenting,* by Gary Thomas, 2004, 2017 Zondervan, Grand Rapics Michigan

*The Connected Child* by Karyn Purvis 2007 McGraw-Hill books

**Podcasts**:
1. Chip Ingram "unstuck" CD and Podcast series at www.livingontheedge.org
2. Tim Keller podcast at www.timothykeller.com

Made in the USA
Columbia, SC
13 April 2019